CALM

in

CHAOS

MINDFULNESS AND MEDITATION
FOR BUSY PROFESSIONALS

THANH NGUYEN

To my husband, Trung Nguyen, who believed in me more than I believed in myself, encouraged me, and cheered me on throughout the writing of this book.

To my children, Valerie and William, who stole my heart from the day you were born: I hope you learn from my experience and use this book as a reminder to cultivate mindfulness, finding calm and happiness in the present moment.

To Eileen Kiera, my Dharma teacher at the Mountain Lamp Community in Deming, WA, for imparting the wisdom of mindfulness practice.

To Sister Rita and Sister Florence, two Franciscan nuns at Kairos House of Prayers in Spokane, Washington, who taught me so much about love and inclusion.

To Sister Dac Nghiem, a Buddhist nun, for enveloping me with love and care whenever I sought refuge at Deer Park Monastery in Escondido, CA.

TABLE OF CONTENTS

"Go and be the change you want to see in the world.
Be a light in the world."
— Sister Florence, Kairos House of Prayers, Spokane, WA

INTRODUCTION

I grew up in post-war Vietnam when it was still a third-world country. The war had destroyed much of the critical infrastructure. We were poor and often without electricity or running water. When I was sixteen, my uncle from America offered to sponsor me to study in the US. It felt like a dream come true, with the potential to transform not only my life but also that of my family. I was thrilled to land in America, a place with so many cars, skyscrapers, and people who looked so different from me. I thought, *Yay! I landed in the land of opportunities*. But within a few weeks, this uncle abused me and kicked me out of his house. My dream was shattered. I was a teenager, unable to speak English, and without money. Though I wanted to go home, I decided to stay and try to make the most of it.

I found a job at a Vietnamese coffee shop, earning much less than minimum wage because it was the only place that would hire me. I studied during the day, worked at night, and wore a headset while sleeping to learn English. For the first few months, I cried myself to sleep every night, but I kept pushing forward.

By 2004, things seemed to be going well. I graduated from the University of California at Berkeley and was three years into my corporate career. I just married the person I love. I no longer had to struggle to earn a living, worry about my immigration status, or yearn for a family. Still, I felt anxious, irritated, and unhappy most of the time. At work, I felt like everyone was against me. At home, I picked fights with my husband and found fault in everything he did. My nervous system, suppressed for so long by the stress of survival and job-hunting, began to unravel. I felt depressed.

Fortunately, a few years earlier, the Zen master Thich Nhat Hanh had visited my university campus, and I had heard of him. I learned that meditation could help solve emotional and mental struggles and make us happier, so I started looking for a meditation practice in the community. I found a group that followed Thich Nhat Hanh's teachings and began attending regularly. A few months later, the group hosted a four-day meditation retreat in Spokane, WA, at Kairos, a house cared for by two Franciscan nuns. We observed silence, self-contemplation, and meditation for most of the days, and the nuns cooked for us. The first two days, I couldn't quiet my mind and found it extremely difficult to sit still. But on day three, something changed. My mind became quieter, and my eyes saw things more clearly and beautifully. As I walked, I started noticing small, beautiful details—the sky seemed bluer, the grass greener, and the birds sang more sweetly. After day four, my husband picked me up, and the first thing he said was, "You seem happier." Over time, he noticed that I had almost become a different person—more cheerful, appreciative, and present. My work relationships also improved. I started noticing the good things happening around me and became more aware of my feelings and emotions. Mindfulness had such a profound impact on me that I continued the practice for over twenty years, sometimes regularly and sometimes not. Whenever I felt unstable, chaotic, or emotionally turbulent, I sought out a Plum Village meditation center, where retreatants follow the teachings of Thich Nhat Hanh, and stayed there. Every single time, the place and the practice helped me heal and restore my spirit.

I have used mindfulness throughout my professional career and found it very useful, from increasing my effectiveness at work and getting along with colleagues to staying calm in stressful situations and leading others well. I documented how I have used mindfulness over the years, and I want to share these practices with you through this small book, hoping it will help you find calm amidst the chaos of life as a busy professional. I hope you enjoy the book. If you do, please share it with others so they can benefit from it as well.

With love,
Thanh Nguyen

WHAT IS MINDFULNESS FOR THE BUSY PROFESSIONAL?

"Mindfulness means paying attention in a particular way: on purpose, in the present moment, and nonjudgmentally."
– Jon Kabat-Zinn

Mindfulness is simply a practice of stopping and looking deeply into what is happening in the present moment without judgment.

There is a Zen story about a person who was riding a horse very quickly through town. A few townspeople became concerned, so they mounted their horses and caught up with him. They asked: "Where are you going?" The horse rider responded: "I don't know. Ask the horse." This story probably made you chuckle, but it is more common than you realize. Nowadays, especially at the workplace, we value being busy. Ask your coworkers how they are doing, and most of the time, you will hear a version of "I'm busy" or "There is so much work to do" or "I have been busy all day today, but feel like I haven't accomplished anything."

Is being busy good for you?

The author Stephen R. Covey, in his book *The 7 Habits of Highly Effective People*, told us to begin with an end in mind. He also shared with us an exercise to figure out what we want to achieve in life. Stephen asked us to visualize our own funeral. At our funeral, three people come up to speak—one from our family, one from our work, and one from our community. What do we want them to talk about? That determines how we should live our lives. I would suggest going a step further: Look at the activities in our days (our busyness) and see if they demonstrate how we want to live our lives. That is how we know where we are going, unlike the rider who told us to ask the horse.

The author, Clayton Christensen, in his book *How Will You Measure Your Life*, shared a story about going to his Harvard reunions. For the first few years after graduation, a lot of people showed up, doing extremely well, with lucrative jobs, fancy houses, and happy families. Then, over the years, fewer and fewer people came to the reunions. As he discovered, the lives of many of these Harvard graduates were falling apart. One was in jail following the Enron scandal; many were facing divorce or had not talked to their children for a long time. He was surprised to discover their situations because he knew these people—they were his classmates. He knew that not only were they intelligent and hard-working, but they also had high ideals for their personal lives and how they could contribute to the world. So, what led them from being high performers with great visions and high ideals to living such unhappy lives and even imprisonment? Could it be because of their habitual energy of being carried from one task to another without stopping and looking deeply to see if the tasks align with how they want to live their lives? Of moving too fast from one thing to the next, of climbing one rung of a ladder after another without knowing if the ladder was leaning against the right wall, of riding the horse but not knowing where it was going?

Mindfulness practice helps us stop, look deeply into what we do, and focus on what matters.

How to practice mindfulness?

It is simple. First, you stop. Then, you take a deep breath in, and breathe out. Then, breathe in and out naturally. As you breathe in, turn your attention to your in-breath. As you breathe out, turn your attention to your out-breath. That is it.

Although the practice sounds simple, it is very difficult. The mind doesn't want to just focus on the in-breath or the out-breath; it wants to multi-task. Doing nothing or just focusing on your breathing seems very unnatural. After a few breaths, you will probably find your mind wandering to other things. When it does and if you recognize it, smile at the thought, and bring your attention back to your breathing.

Now, if you want to help your mind because it definitely doesn't want to and/or cannot practice this simple technique, you can give it another toy to play with. As you breathe in and out, you can recite this poem from the Zen master Thich Nhat Hanh.

"Breathing in,
I know I'm breathing in.
Breathing out,
I know I'm breathing out.
Breathing in,
I calm my body.
Breathing out,
I smile.

In
Out
Calm
Smile."

If you want more ways to practice, you can add a timer and a bell. For every five minutes of practice, you can invite the bell. The sound of the bell can serve as an anchor for your awareness and bring your attention back to your breathing.

Personally, I use an app called Insight Timer. In that app, you can choose how long you want to meditate, and how often you want the bell to sound. You can also select your preferred bell sound. For example: When I meditate for twenty minutes, I can set the bell to sound every five minutes. Every time the bell sounds, it reminds me to come back to my breathing if my mind (as it often does) wanders down the rabbit hole of thoughts.

Okay, so now we know how to practice. How often should we practice?

I recommend as little or as much as you'd like. I often meditate twenty minutes in the morning and twenty minutes at night. Many people meditate for five minutes at a time. When I go on a meditation retreat, I practice longer—for forty-five or sixty minutes at a time and up to ten hours per day. It is entirely up to you. Just five minutes of practice will help you stop, find stillness, and connect with the present moment.

Practicing mindfulness is great, but most of us don't have time to sit and practice all day long. We need a way to carry mindfulness practice into our daily life.

Some examples of how we can practice mindfulness at work and at home:

Writing a technical proposal: One of my early engineering jobs was to write technical proposals for an engineering firm. To prepare, I closed all the windows and applications on my computer (emails, instant messenger, other projects, etc.) that didn't serve the purpose of writing that particular proposal. I put on my noise-canceling headphones because I worked in a cubicle environment, which can sometimes be distracting. I took a deep breath. I listened to my in-breath and out-breath. I paused. As I read the RFQ (Request for

Quotation), I didn't think about reading it quickly to get it done; I didn't think about the email list that was waiting for me. I didn't think about anything except what I was reading. As I read the RFQ, I enjoyed reading it. I underlined important topics; I wrote questions for things I needed to find out and notations for things that I need to go back to. When I wrote the proposal, I approached it the same way. My attention and purpose were on focused on writing that proposal. I wrote it in a way that I thought was best for the customers. I didn't think about home or other projects during that time. Just as during mindfulness meditation practices, I set the time limit for my work to twenty or thirty minutes. Every twenty or thirty minutes, I took a short break from full concentration. I breathed in and breathed out. I walked to get coffee. I looked at others in the office and smiled at them. The result was that I could get my work done faster and with higher quality. If you worked with me and happened to interrupt me during one of those mindful work periods, you would certainly make me jump out of my seat. That is a side effect of being fully immersed in what one is working on.

Talking on the phone: If your job requires you to talk on the phone, whether with a customer, a potential client, or a coworker, you can use the opportunity to bring mindfulness to talking on the phone. Before you pick up the phone, take three deep breaths—breathe in and breathe out, calming, smiling, in and out. As you listen to the other party, you listen with care. You practice listening to the person with all your heart and mind. You don't listen with the intention to reply. You listen with the intention of understanding. Only after you have listened to everything the other person has to say do you speak. As you speak, you rephrase what you heard to make sure you understand the other person correctly. And only after you have received a confirmation of what you heard do you think about your response.

Arriving home: When we arrive home after a long day at work, how often do we rush inside the home, carrying with us the exhaustion, stress, and problems at work? When our children come up and hug us, do we hug them back hastily with a frown still on our face? Or, when we hear them playing loudly or singing, do we yell at them to be quiet? Why do we always bring the past to the present, allowing what happened at work during the day to disturb our time at home with our loved ones? Why do we always bring the future into the present, allowing our worries about the future to ruin the happiness in the present moment? Doing so, we hurt our well-being and the well-being of our family. There are two practices we can use as we arrive home. The first practice is this: Before we enter the home, we stop. We take three deep breaths in and out, and we recite the following verse.

"Breathing in,
Breathing out.
I calm my body,
I smile.

Breathing in,
Breathing out.
I vow to be fully present,

For my loved ones."

Only after doing this will you enter the home. When we enter the home, if our loved ones hug us, we can practice a hugging meditation. In hugging meditation, we don't just quickly hug the person and let go. We hug the person for at least two full breaths. At the first breath, we stop and become fully aware of the hug, enjoying the hug, and feeling the love and warmth of the person hugging us. At the second breath, we can silently say to ourselves, *My dear love, I'm so grateful that you are here with me.*

Mindfulness is a practice. There is not an end to the practice. It is like physical exercise. You don't start practicing running, then stop, and hope that you will continue to stay in shape. You have to continue to practice if you want to maintain your physical fitness.

Mindfulness is a practice of stopping, of looking deeply, of being fully aware of the present moment, not letting the past or the future carry us away, of understanding why you are doing what you are doing. You can and should use mindfulness in everyday applications, from working, leading others, and creating vision and strategy for your company to designing your life and being present for your loved ones.

With the regular practice of stopping and looking deeply, I'm confident you will find lasting joy and happiness.

SCIENTIFIC EVIDENCE ON THE BENEFITS OF MINDFULNESS

"Without data, you're just another person with an opinion."
— W. Edwards Deming

Most chapters in this book dive into the advantages of mindfulness drawn from my own experiences, timeless narratives passed down through centuries of practitioners, and anecdotes. I aim to devote this chapter to sharing several scientific discoveries regarding the benefits of mindfulness.

Mindfulness has gained significant attention in scientific research due to its potential benefits for mental and physical well-being. Here are some key findings from scientific studies:

Reduced Symptoms of Depression and Anxiety: A study published by the Department of Psychology at Stanford University reviewed the magnetic resonance imaging (MRI) scans of sixteen patients and concluded that patients who practiced mindfulness showed evidence of reduced anxiety and depression.[1] Another study by John Hopkins University that included forty-seven trials with more than 3000 participants found that mindfulness moderately improved anxiety and depression after eight weeks.[2]

Improved Cognitive Function: Mindfulness practices have been linked to improvements in cognitive function, including attention, memory, and executive function. Research published in the journal Psychological Science demonstrated that just a couple weeks of mindfulness training can improve attention and working memory.[3]

Enhanced Well-Being and Quality of Life: Mindfulness practices have been associated with increased feelings of well-being and improvements in overall quality of life. A study published by the Department of Psychology and Neuroscience at Duke University shared many benefits of mindfulness, which included increased positive emotions, satisfaction with life, vitality, and effective management of emotions, alongside reduced negative emotions and symptoms of psychological disorders. Additionally, emerging evidence from neurobiological and experimental studies highlights the potential benefits of both inherent mindfulness traits and mindfulness meditation techniques in diminishing emotional reactivity and promoting overall psychological health.[4]

Changes in Brain Structure and Function: Neuroimaging studies have shown that mindfulness practices can lead to changes in brain structure and function, particularly in areas associated with attention, emotion regulation, and self-awareness. Research done by the University of Massachusetts Medical School, Harvard Medical School, and Bender Institute of Neuroimaging in Germany found that mindfulness meditation was associated with increased gray matter density in brain regions involved in learning, memory processes, and emotion regulation.[5]

Pain Management: Mindfulness-based interventions have been shown to be effective in managing chronic pain. Research published in JAMA Internal Medicine found that mindfulness meditation programs were associated with small to moderate reductions in pain severity and pain-related disability.[6]

The discoveries outlined offer convincing proof of the potential advantages of mindfulness spanning mental and physical well-being. Nonetheless, it's crucial to acknowledge that personal encounters with mindfulness can differ. Drawing from my extensive twenty-three-year tenure in the corporate realm as a busy professional, mindfulness practice has been immensely beneficial. Subsequent chapters will explore various ways in which mindfulness can help us in our hectic lives by facilitating the restoration of clarity, tranquility, and purpose to our daily routines.

HOW TO MEDITATE

"Awareness of the breadth is the essence of mindfulness."
– Thich Nhat Hanh

Meditation serves as a means to enhance our mindfulness journey. It's akin to seeking assistance from a personal trainer during intense physical workouts. Yet, the term "meditate" can sometimes evoke intimidation, as if it's exclusive to a select few. In this chapter, I'll explain how effortlessly meditation can become a part of our daily lives.

I recently had the privilege of offering private meditation instruction to a family. At the beginning of the session, the mom had many questions about the goals and techniques of meditation. One of her questions was whether we should keep the mind completely empty and eliminate all thoughts during meditation. I don't think I answered her question well enough because she asked the same question again and reiterated that, according to her reading, if the mind isn't kept completely empty during meditation, the person has failed.

The basis of mindfulness meditation is to be present and aware of what's going on within us. There are multiple techniques that one can use to train one's mind to be present and observing.

One technique is to focus on our breathing and counting our breaths. As you breathe in, you notice an in-breath. As you breathe out, you notice an out-breath, and you begin to count, one. Keep counting your exhalations until you get to ten, and then start over at one. Another technique is to repeat a word. For example: You can use the word "Om" and say it out loud with each out-breath. Take a deep breath in. As you exhale, say the word "Om" out loud.

Another technique is to meditate on a concept, such as the concept of gratefulness. Start repeating this phrase, "Thank you, _____. I wish you well." Fill the space with whomever or whatever happens to jump to your mind without discrimination. Examples are: "Thank you, son. I wish you well. Thank you, sky. I wish you well. Thank you, table. I wish you well. Thank you, pain. I wish you well."

There are other techniques, and some may work well with you while some may work better with others. If you are a beginner, I suggest you pick one technique and try it. I teach the "counting breath" technique. I use this technique and the "meditation on gratefulness" technique interchangeably. All of these techniques serve the same purpose. They help you stay in the present.

During meditation, thoughts will come up. While you are on the count of three breaths, for example, you may remember that you forgot to put out the trash. Or while you say, "Thank you, Mike. I wish you well," you may remember that Mike did something bad to you, and maybe you shouldn't thank him after all. Or while you are in the middle of meditation, you come up with an idea that you find so profound that you can't wait to write it down or share it with others.

Even meditation practitioners who have practiced for many decades still have thoughts coming up during meditation. That is normal. When a thought comes up, acknowledge it. You can say to yourself: *I realize a thought just came up. I can now let it go and resume my practice.* Gently acknowledge it, and then let it go. Do not follow the thought. Do not get up and put the trash out. Do not analyze why Mike did something bad and why you should forgive him or not forgive him. Do not stand up and write down the "profound" ideas. Another thing people do is get mad at the thought: *Jeez . . . I'm trying to meditate, and these thoughts keep creeping up. I can't meditate. I'm not good enough. I will never focus on my breath long enough. I can't keep my mind empty. This effort is ruined.* The angrier you get at the thought, the longer it lingers, and the more you lose your concentration on the present moment. Let it go.

When we think of meditation, we often picture a person

sitting cross-legged on a cushion on the floor, hands placed in front or on their laps, with their eyes half closed. But you don't have to be in that position. You can sit on a chair with your back straight and your feet firmly placed on the ground. If you are petite like me, you can place a cushion at your feet to ensure they are firmly laid flat on a surface and stable.

Another practice of meditation is walking meditation. In walking meditation, we walk gently, putting one foot in front of the other. As we walk, we pay attention to how we place our feet on the ground, noticing our pace, whether it is fast or slow. Typically, we coordinate our breathing with our steps. As we take a step, we breathe in; with the next step, we breathe out. If you walk fast, you can take two steps with every in-breath or out-breath. I practice walking meditation during five-minute breaks at work, in a parking lot, or for an hour on the weekend in the early morning at a nearby park. With every step, I breathe in the fresh air, nourishing my body and mind, and realize how blessed I am to be able to breathe in peace.

Everything in life is impermanent. Our breath is impermanent. Take a deep breath. Try holding it in. See how long you can hold it in. Eventually you must breathe out. An in-breath is impermanent. Once you breathe in, you must breathe out. An out-breath is impermanent. Once you breathe out, you must breathe in. Suffering is impermanent. Suffering comes, and suffering goes away. Think about a period of time in your life when you suffered tremendously and when you thought the suffering would never end. Did the suffering eventually end? Do you feel better now? Happiness also comes and goes. Think about an event that made you happy. Does the happiness last forever?

"Mindfulness is simply being aware of what is happening right now without wishing it were different; enjoying the pleasant without holding on when it changes (which it will); being with the unpleasant without fearing it will always be this way (which it won't)." – James Baraz

The concept of impermanence also applies to meditation. You cannot maintain a state of "no thoughts" or "empty mind" forever. Thoughts will come while you are counting your breaths. Thoughts will come while you try to concentrate. That is okay. When thoughts come, acknowledge them and let them go.

So, what's the goal of meditation, you may ask? How should I feel after meditation?

Countless studies state the benefits of meditation, such as how it alters certain areas of the brain and improves concentration, reduces anxiety, boosts the immune system, etc. For me personally, meditation helps me find peace and calm. Meditation helps me quiet my noisy mind and listen to my heart. Meditation gives me clarity and helps me feel rejuvenated; as a result, it enables me to do more and be more for other people in my life. Whenever I go on multi-day meditation retreats, I always emerge feeling refreshed, more compassionate toward the things and people around me, and more appreciative of the simple things in life. In the words of my family, I come out of meditation retreats a changed woman—a more lovable person, that is.

I'd like to end this chapter with a story Jack Kornfield tells of an old Chinese Zen monk, who, after years of meditation, realized he wasn't enlightened.

He went to the master and said, "Please, may I go find a hut at the top of the mountain and stay there until I finish this practice?" The master, knowing he was ripe, gave his permission.

On the way up the mountain, the monk met an old man walking down, carrying a big bundle. The old man asked, "Where are you going, monk?"

The monk answered, "I'm going to the top of the mountain to sit and either get enlightened or die."

Since the old man looked very wise, the monk was moved to ask him, "Say, old man, do you know anything of this enlightenment?" The old man was really the Bodhisattva Manjusri, who is said to appear to people when they are ready for enlightenment. He let go of his bundle, and it dropped to the ground. As in all good Zen stories, in that moment the monk was enlightened. "You mean it is that simple; just to let go and not grasp anything!"

Then the newly enlightened monk looked back at the old man

and asked, "So now what?" In answer, the old man reached down and picked up the bundle again and walked off toward town.

The concept of impermanence shows up in this story. Being enlightened means being able to let go, to not grasp or attach to anything, and being enlightened means to be able to pick something up again and keep walking on one's journey.

Thoughts come and thoughts go. Events happen and events pass. Breathing in and breathing out.

Happy meditating!

LOVE WHAT YOU DO

"Mindfulness is the art of fully engaging in the present moment with love and curiosity."
— Tara Brach

Many years ago, during a multi-day Zen retreat, I found myself in the kitchen of the Kairos House of Prayers in Spokane, Washington. Tucked away in a secluded area surrounded by acres of pine woods, this small property provided a serene escape from the bustling city life, just minutes away. Stepping into Kairos always feels like shedding the weight of the world. It is a place where life seems to slow down, where the caring presence of Sister Rita and Sister Florence envelop visitors with warmth and hospitality.

As I entered the kitchen, I noticed Sister Rita slicing a tomato. I remarked on the exceptional flavor of the meals over the past few days. Despite their simplicity, the food here always seemed to surpass any culinary experience elsewhere.

Pausing, Sister Rita looked up at me and shared a profound insight: "Dear, I'm cutting this tomato with love. When you approach tasks with love, they tend to turn out wonderfully."

Her words struck a chord within me. Isn't this what we, as Zen practitioners, have spent the last few days at this retreat trying to achieve with our practice? We seek mindfulness in our actions, aiming to free ourselves from the distractions of the past and future, and to immerse our minds fully in the present moment. The present is our reality; the past is but a memory, and the future remains uncertain. Recognizing the beauty of the present moment, we channel our energy and attention into it, infusing it with love and care.

Right then and there, in the Kairos kitchen, I learned a valuable lesson: to approach every task with love. It was a lesson that resonated deeply with the principles of Zen.

So, as we embark on our daily routines as professionals, let us ask ourselves: What tasks will we undertake with love today?

BE A LIGHT IN THE WORLD

"Sometimes your joy is the source of your smile,
but sometimes your smile can be the source of your joy."
— Thich Nhat Hanh

Sunday, November 6, 2017, a group of us was finishing up a multi-day meditation retreat. Our group of Zen meditation practitioners had been there for four days. During those four days, our schedule included long periods of sitting meditation, walking meditation, working meditation, eating meditation, and free-time periods where we often wandered alone in the beautiful nature. After several full days of complete silence, surrounded by chirping birds, fresh wild animal footprints, and the smell of the pine wood where we were staying, I felt so much peace, love, and joy.

The last meal of our retreat was an informal lunch, during which everyone was allowed to talk so we could get to know each other a little bit before departing on our own way and say our goodbyes. I felt so much love and peace. Everyone

27

felt the same way. We appreciated each other, appreciated this world and all the goodness that it has to offer. The smiles, the laughter and the chatting were joyously resonating all around me.

About this time, Sister Florence came out. She was one of the two Catholic nuns who cared for that place and had been cooking for us during the retreat. Sister Florence and Sister Rita were two of the kindest, most loving, most caring, and upbeat people I had ever known. They always greeted us with the warmest, brightest smiles and the tightest hugs. Sister Florence had even sung for us to say goodbye during our previous retreats there. The sisters taught me to do things with mindfulness, do things with love and with heart, more than any Zen practice could have taught me. Sister Florence came out with teary eyes and told us about the shooting inside a church in Sutherland Springs, Texas.

Our hearts broke. We didn't know what to say. The tragedy was too much to bear, and the fact that the killer struck inside a church where people gather for worship, for fellowship, for love was too much to accept.

After the love and joy that we experienced, we were brought back to the reality of life that there was still so much pain, suffering, and sadness in this world.

I could feel her pain. I could feel everyone's pain. In place of the laugher and chatting that was going on a few minutes earlier, it was a dreaded silence.

Sister Florence spoke again: "I so appreciated the time you spent here over the last few days with us. We need more peace and love in this world. We need more people like you. Go and be the change you want to see in the world. Be a light in the world."

She was right. Each of us has the potential to be a light in the world. Each of us has the intelligence and the resourcefulness to make a positive difference. If you think not, think about the last time someone smiled at you when you needed it most; think about the last time someone gave you a hug and comforted you. Think about someone saying something encouraging to you and lifting you up. Can you be that person to others?

As for me, I walked away thinking about what I could do. Her words sank in. What can I do to be the change and a light in the world? And a light bulb formed. I had experienced so much love and joy in the last few days. I could share this meditation practice with others. Meditation helped me greatly, and I had practiced it for many years. I knew it could be a great instrument to help individuals find joy, peace, and love. I found a studio and started meditation classes for the community. Several groups came and practiced regularly. It gave me so much joy to see how relaxed people felt after each session. I knew I was doing a small part toward being the change I want to see in the world.

Being a light in the workplace involves embodying qualities that uplift and inspire those around you. Here are some ways to achieve this:

Maintain a positive outlook, even in challenging situations. Just as our breath flows in and out, so too do challenging moments come and go. One cannot hold onto an in-breath or an out-breath forever. Similarly, challenging situations shall pass. Remember that our optimism can be contagious, contributing to a more pleasant work environment.

Show empathy toward your colleagues by mindfully listening to their concerns and offering support when needed. Compassion fosters a sense of connection and camaraderie among team members.

Treat everyone with kindness and respect, regardless of their position or background. Small acts of kindness, such as expressing gratitude or helping, can go a long way toward brightening someone's day.

Interact mindfully with your coworkers by attentively acknowledging their accomplishments and difficulties. Embrace their successes with genuine celebration and offer uplifting encouragement during moments of setback.

Practice meditation to calm the noise in your mind, allowing you to come up with creative ideas. When your brain is cluttered with distractions, worries, or constant chatter, it can be challenging to tap into your creative potential. Creating a calm mental space allows you to access your imagination more freely, enabling innovative ideas to emerge.

Strive for personal and professional growth by continuously learning and developing new skills. Share your knowledge and experiences with others and encourage a culture of lifelong learning within the workplace.

By embodying these qualities and behaviors, you can be a beacon of light in the workplace, inspiring and uplifting those around you to strive for excellence and create a positive and fulfilling work environment.

What will you do today to be a light in the world?

LEAD WITH OPEN-MINDEDNESS

*"In the beginner's mind there are many possibilities,
but in the expert's there are few."*
– Shunryu Suzuki

A long time ago, there was a famous Zen master. People from all over the country came to visit him, hoping to learn from him and ask him for advice. One time, a prominent military leader came to visit. With great authority, he told the Zen master: "I came here to discuss life philosophy with you. Tell me what defines a good life." The master smiled and asked the gentleman to come back the next morning when they could discuss that over a cup of tea. The next morning, when tea was served, the Zen master picked up the teapot and started pouring into the tiny teacup in front of the military leader. He kept pouring even when tea was overflowing all over the tray. The military leader got really annoyed and yelled: "Stop! Don't you see the tea is spilling all over?"

The Zen master looked up and replied: "You are like this teacup, so full of preconceived notions. How can I add anything more to you? Come back when you are truly ready to listen with an empty mind."

Although this was a Zen story and took place a long time ago, it rings true today. How often do we listen with the intent to respond? How often do we ask someone for their opinion but do not actually care for it? How often do we come to a brainstorming session with all the answers, sure that our answers are the best ones? As a leader, is it our job to have all the answers? What does it mean when our cup of tea is so full that we cannot take in new tea? On the other hand, will we pour tea into someone's cup when it is already full?

In the bustling world of modern professionals, the Zen master's tale resonates profoundly, serving as a timeless reminder of the pitfalls of a closed mind and the virtues of an open one. As we navigate through the complexities of our careers and personal lives, it's all too easy to find ourselves resembling the military leader—brimming with certainties, preconceptions, and the relentless pursuit of productivity.

In the Zen master's simple act of pouring tea, we witness a profound metaphor for the state of our mind. How often do we approach interactions and discussions with our mental teacups already overflowing with assumptions and judgments? How frequently do we find ourselves more focused on formulating our responses than truly absorbing what others have to offer?

As leaders, the pressure to have all the answers can be immense. We're expected to provide guidance, make decisions, and chart the course forward. Yet, in our quest for certainty and control, we risk overlooking the invaluable insights and perspectives that lie beyond the confines of our own teacups.

True leadership, as the Zen master suggests, requires the humility to recognize the limitations of our knowledge and the willingness to embrace the wisdom that emerges from an open mind. It's about creating space for diverse viewpoints, fostering a culture of collaboration, and acknowledging that innovation thrives in the fertile soil of shared dialogue and mutual respect.

But the lesson extends beyond the realm of leadership—it speaks to the essence of mindful living. Just as a teacup overflowing with tea cannot hold any more, a mind cluttered with preconceptions and attachments cannot truly experience the richness of the present moment. As the Zen master Thich Nhat Hanh said, "Usually when we hear or read something new, we just compare it to our own ideas. If it is the same, we accept it and say that it is correct. If it is not, we say it is incorrect. In either case, we learn nothing." Mindfulness invites us to cultivate the art of emptying our cups, releasing the burden of excessive mental baggage, and embracing each moment with curiosity and openness.

So, let us heed the wisdom of the Zen master as we navigate the complexities of our professional and personal lives. Let us approach each interaction, each decision, with the humility of an empty cup, ready to receive the gifts of insight and understanding that await us. For it is in the space of an open mind that true growth, innovation, and fulfillment unfold.

FIND OUR "WHY"

"Everyone has his own specific vocation or mission in life; everyone must carry out a concrete assignment that demands fulfillment. Therein he cannot be replaced, nor can his life be repeated. Thus, everyone's task is as unique as his specific opportunity to implement it."
– Viktor Frankl

In the hectic whirlwind of our professional lives, it's easy to find ourselves swept away by the relentless demands of work. We spend the majority of our waking hours engaged in the pursuit of our careers, and even during our precious moments of respite, thoughts of work often linger at the forefront of our minds. For many, work serves as a source of joy, fulfillment, and purpose—a platform that allows us to express our talents and make a meaningful impact on the world. Yet, amid the triumphs and achievements, there are inevitably moments when the weight of our responsibilities bears down upon us, threatening to overwhelm our spirit.

In times of challenge and adversity, it's essential to pause and reflect on the fundamental question: Why do we work? Viktor Frankl, the renowned Holocaust survivor and psychologist, famously asserted that understanding our "why" can provide us with the resilience and fortitude to weather any storm. Mindfulness offers us a pathway to explore this question with clarity and insight, guiding us to uncover the deeper motivations and aspirations that drive our professional endeavors.

At first glance, the most immediate answer may seem straightforward: We work to earn a living, to support ourselves and our loved ones, to meet our material needs and obligations. Yet, as we delve beneath the surface, we discover that our reasons for working extend far beyond mere financial gain. Money serves as a means to an end—a vessel through which we pursue higher aspirations such as happiness, fulfillment, and personal growth.

Maslow's hierarchy of needs provides a framework for understanding the multifaceted nature of our motivations. Maslow describes five rungs of human needs:

- The bottom rung is physiological needs—the needs for food, air, water, and shelter.

- The second rung is safety-related needs—the needs to be healthy and to be secure.

- The third rung is the need to feel loved, to feel we belong with a family and a community.

- The fourth rung is the need to feel respected.

- And the highest rung that every human aspires to reach (whether he knows it or not) is self-actualization—the innate drive to realize our fullest potential and make a meaningful contribution to the world. Mindfulness invites us to explore the layers of our being, guiding us to align our actions with our deepest values and aspirations.

We often mistake the means for the end. We chase money and fame, trying to climb up the corporate ladder, stepping on one another, but we sacrifice the relationships at work, forgo our time with family, neglect our health, and forget the deeper reason of why we work. It is important for each of us to take the time to think about and internalize why we work.

Mindfulness, the practice of being present and fully engaged with the current moment, can be a powerful tool to explore and understand our motivations for working. By applying mindfulness to this inquiry, we gain deeper insights into our values and goals and the emotional and psychological reasons behind our work.

Start by finding a quiet and comfortable place where you can sit without distraction. Begin your session by setting a clear intention: *I am here to look deeply and understand why I work*. Take a few deep breaths, in and out, to anchor yourself in the present moment. Allow thoughts and feelings about work to arise naturally. Observe these thoughts without trying to change or judge them. Notice any emotions, physical sensations, or images that come to mind when you think about work. Gently ask yourself the following questions:

- What are my primary motivations for working?

- How does my work align with my passion and talents?

- What makes me cry, causes me pain, or gives me joy at work?

- What are the rewards and challenges associated with my work?

Acknowledge whatever thoughts, feelings, or sensations arise. Accept them as they are, without judgment. This acceptance is key to understanding your true motivations and feelings about work. You may want to keep a journal nearby to write down your thoughts and feelings. The practice of writing helps to clarify your insights and make them more concrete.

The why within each of us is different. I work because it fuels my desire for learning and helps me grow. I work because through my work I can contribute to making the world a better place. I work because I love the people I work with and believe I can make a positive difference in their lives. When one of these three conditions is threatened, I feel thrown off balance. Then, it is time for me to re-evaluate my path. Do I still have opportunities to learn and grow at work? Do I still believe in the mission of the company? Do I believe that my work helps make the world a better place? Do I still have opportunities to encourage my team and help them maximize their potential?

Your why will be different than mine, but understanding your why will help you overcome difficult times at work and help you decide whether to stay or leave. At the end of life, no one wants to regret that they have spent most of their life working in the wrong place or having the wrong career.

As we journey through the maze of our careers, let us remember the words of wisdom passed down through the ages: "Know thyself." By cultivating mindfulness and self-awareness, we unlock the door to our innermost truths, discovering the profound purpose and meaning that infuse every aspect of our work.

Many years ago, I met a young rising star at work. One day, I asked how she was doing, and her reply puzzled me. She said, "I'm surviving the rat race." Really! Is that all there is to work? A rat race. The sound of it is not appealing. I would like my work to mean more than that; I don't think I want to win a race that has the word "rat" in it.

In the words of one of my mentors, "We are spiritual beings inhabiting human bodies." Our souls yearn for a deeper sense of purpose and connection, transcending the materialistic pursuits of the world. Mindfulness invites us to awaken to this larger purpose, guiding us to infuse our work with meaning and significance that extends far beyond the confines of the corporate rat race.

There is a parable about three bricklayers. The first bricklayer, when asked what he was doing, replied, "I'm

41

laying bricks." The second bricklayer said, "I'm building a wall." The third bricklayer replied with a gleam in his eyes, "I'm building a cathedral that will be a place of healing for millions of people."

Which bricklayer are you?

Martin Luther King, Jr. once observed, "If it falls your lot to be a street sweeper, sweep streets like Michelangelo painted pictures, sweep streets like Beethoven composed music, sweep streets like Leontyne Price sings before the Metropolitan Opera. Sweep streets like Shakespeare wrote poetry. Sweep streets so well that all the hosts of heaven and earth will have to pause and say: Here lived a great street sweeper who swept his job well."

Understanding why you work will help you be the person that all the hosts of heaven and earth will have to pause and say: Here is a person who has done her job well.

Mindfulness allows us to understand deeply the motivations that guide us to align our actions with our values and intentions, empowering us to do our best work with presence and meaning.

HANDLE DIFFICULT PEOPLE

*"When another person makes you suffer, it is because he suffers
deeply within himself, and his suffering is spilling over.
He does not need punishment; he needs help."*
— Thich Nhat Hanh

During our careers, regardless of our role or the companies we work for, we inevitably encounter difficult situations that we must navigate. Difficult people at work are individuals who consistently exhibit challenging behaviors that hinder productivity and create a negative work environment. These individuals may display traits such as aggression, stubbornness, or a lack of cooperation, making it difficult for us to effectively collaborate and achieve common goals.

In my experience, dealing with difficult individuals has been challenging, but I have found a few helpful strategies.

First, I go back to my core values, which include love and courage. For example, I once encountered a loud and confrontational customer while working at his house. Initially,

I was unsure how to handle his aggressive behavior, but because I have a deep love for my team, I found the courage to confront this customer, calmly address the situation, and defuse it. In that moment, I also reminded myself of the love I have for the customer, thinking that this person must be dealing with his own struggles, which may have contributed to his behavior. Later, when his wife and children arrived home and began yelling at him in the same manner he had done to us, it became clear that because our project was going to take longer than expected, he was under a lot of pressure and was likely worried about getting yelled at himself. Therefore, he lashed out at us. Understanding this helped me feel more empathetic towards him instead of getting angry. In situations like these, it is important to remember that difficult people often have their own underlying issues and insecurities that contribute to their behavior. By approaching them with empathy and understanding, we can create a more positive and productive work environment.

Second, I remember my "why." As Viktor Frankl, a Holocaust survivor, once said, "One who has a 'why' to live for can endure almost any 'how.'" There were times when I had to work over 100 hours a week for months on end, sacrificing time with my family and my health. I also traveled to sites weekly and was away from my children. On top of that, I had to deal with a difficult senior leader from our client who constantly tried to undermine our project and our credibility, casting doubts about our capability and competencies. During one particularly difficult week, I was on site during my children's spring break, and this person was critical and condescending. I ran to the car because I couldn't hold back my tears. I sat there and cried. In that moment, I questioned why I had to push myself so hard and endure such difficult people. But then, I remembered my "why." I was there because I was a good leader who loved and cared for my team and was committed to our important mission of providing safe and reliable electricity generation and clean energy. This reminder helped me stay focused on the bigger picture and handle the situation with more grace.

Third, I take stock of my backup options. Sometimes, we get so caught up in a difficult moment that we forget to consider other options, so I make a conscious effort to think about the ultimate outcome if my current situation doesn't work. This means considering my financial stability and knowing that I can leave my job at any time if necessary. I am there because I genuinely enjoy my work and the people, not because I am obligated to be there. I also remind myself of my valuable skills and experience, knowing that I can find a new job whenever I choose to leave. This helps me feel unstuck and gives me a sense of freedom, peace, and confidence to handle challenging situations and difficult individuals.

Lastly, I remember to breathe. When a difficult person says something untrue or provokes a strong emotional response in me, I take a deep breath. This helps me calm down and creates some space between my emotions and my response, allowing me to think more clearly and respond appropriately. I also draw upon my Zen practice and remember that everything is impermanent in this life. This situation shall pass. Life is short, so it's our responsibility to not waste time being upset over things that are outside our control but to spend that time focusing on adding value and making an impact.

I hope these strategies are helpful to you. Every situation is unique, and it may take time and repetition to find what works best for you.

While dealing with difficult people and challenging situations can be exhausting and emotionally draining, it is important to act according to our core values, remembering the purpose and the impact we are making. By staying focused on our "why" and reminding ourselves of our worth and options, we can navigate these situations with grace and confidence. Taking a moment to breathe and practice mindfulness also helps us maintain clarity and respond appropriately. Ultimately, finding strategies that work for us individually is key to overcoming these challenges and achieving success in our personal and professional lives.

By implementing these strategies and staying true to ourselves, we can not only handle difficult individuals and situations, but we can grow and thrive in the process. Remember, it is through these challenges that we develop resilience, strengthen our skills, and become better versions of ourselves. So, embrace the opportunities for growth and continue to navigate the complexities of life with determination and a positive mindset.

LOVE YOURSELF

"Be kinder to yourself.
And then let your kindness flood the world."
– Pema Chödrön

As human beings, we constantly face challenges, which I call the storms of life. These can be anything from losing a job to losing a loved one. With so many layoffs happening in the year 2023, the example I use below is associated with facing a job loss, but the same concept can be applied to other unfortunate events in life.

A job loss can be devastating. Aside from possibly causing financial hardship, many of us seek answers. Why me? What are the selection criteria? Am I the casualty of an automatic algorithm or political infighting? For most of us, our identity is tied to our jobs, and being let go seems like a loss of identity. How am I going to introduce myself when people ask what I'm doing? Is it okay to say, "I'm in transition" or "I'm a stay-at-home parent"? Will I be deemed a failure for not having a job? The blow of a job loss is especially hard for high performers who pour their heart into work and contribute above and beyond what is expected of them. For those who are still seeking the answers, I'm pretty sure you are not going to find them externally. Deep inside your heart, you already know the answers.

There is a Zen parable about the two arrows. Picture yourself walking through the forest, enjoying the fresh air and the lustrous greenery around you. Suddenly, you get hit by an arrow that causes tremendous physical pain. This first arrow already happened and is inevitable; it represents an unfortunate event that happens to us in life, like sickness, injury, death, or loss of employment. Like the weather, these events are beyond our control. No one can control the weather. Hurricanes and storms come, and we can't stop them. But the way we react determines how fast and how well we recover. The unexpected misfortune is the first arrow that hits us, and how we react to it can be the second arrow. Often, as soon as the first arrow hits, we immediately reach for the second arrow to inflict upon ourselves. When we repeatedly replay a bad event in our head with anguish, fear, and self-doubts, we add pain and suffering to the wound of the first arrow. It's like we are stabbing the same wound again and again, thus making it hard to heal. In the example of losing a job, we may question ourselves about what we did wrong, telling ourselves that we weren't good enough or even that we may never be able to get a job again. That turns into the fear of not being able to provide medical care and put food on the table for the family. When we are so overpowered by this habitual energy of hurting ourselves with the second arrow, we don't have the energy to find a constructive solution.

So, how do we avoid this? The past is already gone. There is nothing we can do to change the past. Questioning it and thinking about it won't change it. At some point in the future, when our emotional reaction to the event lessens, we can come back to it to learn how we might do better. But, in the meantime, while emotion is still high, it's best to leave the event alone. In mindfulness, we practice observing the feelings. When we sense the rising of emotions such as sadness, frustration, fear, or anger, we acknowledge that we are feeling sad, frustrated, fearful, or angry. When we replay the event in our head, we are aware of our thoughts. By being aware of our thoughts and emotions, we can control how we respond to the event and control our actions in such a way that frees us and moves us forward to the next step.

Here is a practice that can help us redirect our focus in those situations. As we become aware of rising painful emotions, we turn our attention to our breath. When we breathe in, we know we are breathing in. When we breathe out, we know we are breathing out. Our breaths can serve as an anchor to help soothe the strong negative emotions and bring us back to the present moment. Our breath can be shallow and rapid, or deep and slow, depending on our mood and emotions at the time. Just observe it.

My teacher helps me practice a Gatha, which is a chant.

When breathing in and out, I focus on the in-breath and the out-breath while repeating the Gatha. Just a few minutes of doing this practice can help restore calm and peace.

"Breathing in, I know I'm breathing in
Breathing out, I know I'm breathing out
Breathing in, I notice my in-breath grows deep
Breathing out, I notice my out-breath goes slow

In
Out
Deep
Slow

Breathing in, I calm my body
Breathing out, I smile
Dwelling in the present moment
I know it's a wonderful moment

Calm
Smile
Present moment
Wonderful moment." – Thich Nhat Hanh

Walking meditation in nature, combined with sitting meditation, can accelerate healing. Nature has a wonderful soothing effect on our soul. Go to a park, touch the grass, and breathe in the fresh air. As we take each step, notice how the ground beneath us feels and how fast or slow our steps are. As we walk and breathe, we can continue reciting the Gatha above, allowing its calming words to guide our mind and deepen our connection to the present moment. This practice not only grounds us physically but also nurtures our emotional and mental well-being.

The past is already gone. The future is not yet here. We have only the present moment, and we can control our actions in the present moment to lessen the pain from the past, to be constructive and help our future. Let's not stab ourselves with the second arrow. The first arrow is painful enough, but the second arrow can cause even more pain.

Marcus Aurelius said, "It's time you realized that you have something in you more powerful and miraculous than the things that affect you and make you dance like a puppet." Our breath is the thing that is always present, powerful, and miraculous. It is the anchor to help us stop the habitual energy of stabbing ourselves with the second arrow. When we can stop, we can rest, gradually recover, and gain clarity to decide how to move forward.

BLOSSOM BEYOND ADVERSITY

"The lotus flower blooms most beautifully
from the deepest and thickest mud."
– Thich Nhat Hanh

During a leadership development class, as I was teaching that the best way to make a positive impact is to add value to others, a participant commented: "It's so hard to add value to people who hate us."

In our professional lives, we so often work with people who are for us and others who seem to be against us. We tend to take sides and do more for people whom we like and do less or make it difficult for those we don't like. While this is a common attitude, it is detrimental to our professional growth and the success of the organizational objectives. In order to achieve success, we need everyone to work together toward a common goal. So, how do we add value to people who seem to be against us? Perhaps a lesson from the lotus will help.

Have you ever marveled at the grace of a lotus flower? Despite emerging from the murky depths of mud, it blossoms with unparalleled beauty, exuding a fragrance that captivates all who encounter it. The lotus teaches us a profound lesson in resilience and selflessness.

Unlike many of us, the lotus does not discriminate in its offerings. It doesn't withhold its beauty from those it deems unworthy, nor does it shower its beauty on those it favors. Instead, it serves everyone with equal fervor, simply because that is its nature.

In the same way, we too can rise above our adversities and trials to become sources of inspiration and positivity in the world. Our struggles and setbacks need not define us; rather, they can fuel our growth and fortify our character.

Our individual journeys, marked by hardship and triumph alike, become invaluable resources for others navigating similar paths. And even when faced with criticism or jealousy from others, we continue to extend our hand in service, recognizing that we serve others because of who we are, not because of who they are. Our true purpose lies in uplifting those around us.

Just as the lotus is destined to bloom and spread its beauty, we too are meant to shine and contribute meaningfully to the world. Let us embrace our inherent potential for greatness and strive to make a positive difference.

FOCUS ON THE BIGGER PICTURE

"I reached the pinnacle of success in the business world. In others' eyes my life is an epitome of success. At this moment, lying on the sickbed and recalling my whole life, I realize that all the recognition and wealth that I took so much pride in have paled and become meaningless in the face of impending death."
– Steve Jobs

In the 1600s, Gudo Toshoku was a well-known Zen master in Japan. His practice was so great that he became the teacher of the retired Japanese emperor, Go-Yozei. Because Gudo liked to travel throughout Japan to visit Zen temples, almost everyone in Japan knew his name and gave him much respect. One day, he stopped at a village and found an inn where he would spend the night. Seeing how sad the wife of the innkeeper was, he asked her what happened. The wife responded: "My husband, he isn't here. When he drinks, he loses his temper and comes home to beat me and our children. I have talked to him many times and begged him to stay away from the alcohol, but he doesn't listen to me. I don't know what to do any more."

Gudo told the wife: "Let me see how I can help. You can go to bed. I'll sit here to meditate and wait for your husband. Just leave me with food and drink for your husband, and let me take it from here."

Late in the evening, the husband came home very drunk, yelling for food and drink. Gudo calmly told the man: "Your family went to sleep already. On the table, there is food and drink. You can help yourself." The man helped himself and then fell asleep at the table.

In the morning, when the husband woke up, he was embarrassed and surprised to see a Zen master sitting across from him in a relaxed and meditative posture. Gudo told the man: "You are awake now. I'm going back to the capital. My name is Gudo."

Upon hearing Gudo's name, the man knelt on the floor and begged for forgiveness. Gudo went on to say: "Human life is very short. Life changes suddenly. If you keep getting yourself drunk like that, how do you have time to take care of yourself and your family, and how do you do the other important things?"

The husband broke into tears and offered to carry Gudo's bag for three miles. After three miles, he asked to carry it for another two miles. And again at the end of the next two miles, he asked to carry it for five more miles. Finally, he asked Gudo if he could follow him to learn Zen practices. This husband later became one of the most famous Zen masters of Japan. His name was Shido Munan.

When drunk, the mind and judgment are dimmed and misguided. We lose the capacity to understand what is truly important, and we don't focus on what matters. We bring sorrows to ourselves and others.

Most of us are not guilty of being drunk on alcohol, but are we drunk in other aspects of life, such as the social pecking order, winning vs. losing, being right or wrong, fame and fortune? The effect is the same as being drunk on alcohol. Fame and fortune blind our mind and impair our judgment. Caring too much about winning or losing or about being right or wrong can make us forget the end goal. How often do we let the pecking order (job title or social ranking) stop us from speaking up and voicing truths? Or even worse, how often do people act aggressively, intimidating, abusing, or harassing others merely to elevate their own social status and their own sense of self- importance?

I am not saying we should drop what we're doing and become Zen masters like Gudo and Munan. But should we stop for a moment to think about how we conduct our lives and understand what truly matters? We should not let the materialistic, superficial things blind us as if we were drunk.

In a company, if an individual cares too much about his own reputation and recognition, and if he puts too much emphasis on self-promotion, the company cannot succeed. President Truman said it best: "It's amazing what you can accomplish when you do not care who gets the credit." I participated in projects where team members had one another's back and cared for others genuinely. Behind the scene, they reminded each other of what needs to get done without paying attention to who gets the credit. They supported and carried a teammate's load when it was needed. They focused on the end goal. When a person represented the team in public, others privately reminded that person of what she needed to remember or may have missed. In this type of environment, it doesn't matter how difficult the project is; chances are high that this team would succeed.

It bothers me when a person proclaims, "I alone did this or that" and puts other team members down and criticizes them behind their backs. When individuals in a team put emphasis on getting recognition for themselves, the team will not succeed. We need to remember that in this world, no one wins alone. We are inter-dependent. Don't let fame and pride blind thoughts and actions. Don't be like a drunk person.

Clayton Christensen, a professor at Harvard University and the author of many bestsellers such as *The Innovator's Dilemma* and *The Innovator's Solution*, said in his book *How will you measure your life?*, "Don't worry about the level of prominence you have achieved; worry about the individuals you have helped become better people. This is my final recommendation: Consider the metric by which your life will be judged, and resolve to live every day so that in the end, your life will be judged a success."

Clayton described many of his Harvard classmates at a class reunion. Despite gaining early success in the workplace, in the end they had experienced terrible setbacks such as prison, divorce or even suicide. It was because they had chosen the wrong yardstick and climbed a ladder leaning on the wrong wall. In a sense, these classmates were drunk. They were drunk not with alcohol but with social metrics like fame, power, and fortune.

Most misfortunes in life come from our attachments to false things. We are attached to negative habits. We are attached to the pecking order, win or lose, being right or wrong, fame and fortune. But can we bring any of that to the graveyard? On our deathbed, the only thing that will matter is how we lived our lives to add value to others.

PRACTICE NONATTACHMENT

"Letting go gives us freedom,
and freedom is the only condition for happiness."
– Thich Nhat Hanh

How are you feeling at this particular moment? Happy? Sad? Frustrated? Angry? A lot of what we feel has to do with how we react to a situation or how attached we become to a certain way of thinking or a certain set of outcomes.

Why are we so attached to a certain way of thinking or a certain set of outcomes? Some people are attached to wealth, and the outcome of a situation may affect their financial status. Some people are attached to their self-image, and so when they learn that there is a different way to do things, it hurts their ego. Some people are attached to social status, and a different way of thinking or a different outcome may alter their social standing. Some are so in love that a change to the relationship may hurt them deeply, or if we lose someone we love, we certainly feel grief and sadness.

In this chapter, I will attempt to address several issues of attachments.

Attachment to wealth and social status: As we climb the social ladder and hold on to our pride and ego, we should take a minute to pause and think about the goal. All of us will, one day, arrive at the same destination—the graveyard. All we can possess then is a few feet of earth. People may miss us and think of us for a little while, but inevitably, they will move on with their lives. So, as you see, we actually hold on to nothing. We are merely stewards of the social status or the wealth that is temporarily in our hands. All that we have and hold on to will go away. The only thing that will last is the legacy that we leave behind. Imagine attending your own funeral where a person from your family, a person from your work, a person from your friendship circle, and a person in your community step up to talk about you. What do you want them to say?

The truth is that we do not have absolute control over our wealth or social status. All of that can go away with a change in the political environment and the financial market. In 1975, after the Vietnam War, many wealthy, high-ranking members of the former Vietnamese government experienced this change. Before the war, they might have been rich and held high social status. But after the war, their wealth and social status were stripped, and the only thing they had left was their ability to persevere in their thoughts and actions. Many of these people survived the challenge, immigrated to the United States, built a successful new life, and became valuable citizens of their new country. Dr. Viktor Frankl, an Austrian psychologist, experienced this, when in one day, he lost his wife and parents in a concentration camp. He said when everything is taken from a man, only one thing remains —our ability to choose our attitude in any circumstance. Dr. Frankl taught us, instead of being attached to things, our life's meaning comes from three sources: purposeful work, love, and courage in the face of difficulty.

In the grand scheme of things, we have little control over our wealth and social status. All of that can disappear in a moment. So, really, all of our attachment to wealth, social status or ego is a waste of time and effort. Instead, ask: What can we do in this moment to add value to the people around us? What can we do to help make this world a better place? What can we do to give back so that we do not waste the space and the earth's resources that nourish us?

Attachment to health and relationships: One of our deepest fears the fear of bad health, death, and losing our loved ones. Although I am not afraid of death, I love my children and husband so much that I am afraid to think of death, as it will separate me from them. However, despite all my efforts, we all grow and change. As my children grow older, they spend less and less time with me, and eventually, the day will come when we shall part, either by death or other circumstances. Holding onto them will not help. Trying to exert control over them will do more harm in the long run. Instead, I should try to love in such a way that the person I love feels free. Regarding health, no matter how much we care for our health, illness will come. Accepting the inevitable reduces my fear and anxiety.

Below is a poem from the Zen master Thich Nhat Hanh that I recite daily during my meditation.

"I am of the nature to grow old.
There is no way to escape growing old.

I am of the nature to have ill health.
There is no way to escape ill health.

I am of the nature to die.
There is no way to escape death.

All that is dear to me and everyone I love are of the nature to change.
There is no way to escape being separated from them.

My actions are my only true belongings.
I cannot escape the consequences of my actions.
My actions are the ground upon which I stand."

We have no control over our health or the people we love; all we have control over is our actions. So, we should ensure that our actions bring love and kindness and add value to the people we love and the world around us.

Attachment to ego: Although I mentioned ego in the section about attachment to wealth and social status, I think it deserves its own section. One of the major causes of pain and suffering is the need to be right. We assume that our way is the best way, and other ways are not as good or are wrong. Even worse, when someone does something that affects us the wrong way, we assume that they are either out to get us, or they are stupid. Why is that?

We all know ego is bad for us. It prevents us from working collaboratively and being open-minded to new ideas. It impedes progress and limits our personal growth. It creates unrealistic entitlements; thus when those are not met, we get hurt. Yes, we all fall into the trap of ego and find ourselves justifying why we are right and claiming that others are "out to get us."

Here are a few tactics that work for me to recognize when ego takes place and to take steps to curb it.

In a conversation or discussion, when I stop hearing or comprehending what the other person is saying, that's when ego starts taking over. When I feel my heart constricted or an emotion rising, that's when my ego is taking over. Being able to identify those cues helps me take actions to stop it from getting out of hand. To address my own ego, I do the following: First, I take a few deep breaths to center myself and get back into the deep listening mode; then I ask questions to understand the other person's point of view, and I ask myself what would be the harm if I followed that person's recommendations even when I don't agree. Finally, I give the other person the benefit of the doubt and think of them as my friend. Together, we are trying to find a win-win solution. In Zen practice, there is something called the middle way. The middle way is a way of life—it teaches that there is not one absolute right or wrong. It is not going forward, going backward, or standing still. It's being in the present moment, listening deeply, letting nature take its course, then finding our way around it, nudging and adding value along the way. As with many things in life, there is not one straight line to get from point A to point B or from one milestone to the next. Often, the fastest way is not the straight line. Those who climb Mount Everest can attest to this. If they attempt a straight path from base camp to summit, they will never arrive. With a work team or with friends and family members, what matters is not how fast we get there, but how far we can go together. An African proverb says this best: "If you want to go fast, go alone. If you want to go far, go together."

Our universe continues to expand; our world is evolving; every day, new technologies and new ways of doing things come out. Being set on one idea or having a big ego prevents us from learning and adapting to the ever-increasing pool of opportunities. Attachments to fame, wealth, ego, things, or people cause us suffering. In the grand scheme of things, we have very little control over how things turn out. We can't bring our fame and wealth with us to the graveyard. We and the people we love possess the nature to change. The only thing we have control over is our thoughts and actions in the present moment. Those thoughts and actions can create a positive impact on the people around us and help us leave behind a better world than we found. I want to leave you with you one last thought from the Quaker monk, Étienne de Grellet, "I shall pass this way but once; any good that I can do or any kindness I can show to any human being; let me do it now. Let me not defer nor neglect it, for I shall not pass this way again."

Let's focus on adding value and helping others.

EMBRACE POSITIVITY

"Amidst the mud of suffering, let us bloom as lotuses, embracing both the pain and the beauty of life."
– Unknown

Thich Nhat Hanh once said, "Everyone knows we need to have mud for lotuses to grow. The mud doesn't smell so good, but the lotus flower smells very good. If you don't have mud, the lotus won't manifest. You can't grow lotus flowers on marble. Without mud, there can be no lotus... If you know how to make good use of the mud, you can grow beautiful lotuses."

I asked my Dharma teacher at the time: "Teacher, life has so much suffering. I cannot stop my tears when I meditate, and my thoughts turn to the pain and suffering of people. There is suffering all around me, from my own family members to the people in the world. Millions of children don't have enough food. Many people are still living under constant bombing, attacks, fighting, killing, and fear. There is still oppression where people cannot be free, do not have the opportunity for an education, do not have access to clean water or basic human necessities. There is so much pain. Whenever I turn on the news, something horrible has happened. How can I stay informed, be aware of my surrounding, of people's emotions and feelings, and be compassionate without being pulled into the sea of suffering myself? I want to open my heart to people, but that means being vulnerable to disappointment and to pain. A heart is a fragile thing. A heart can love and laugh easily, but it can also ache easily. Sometimes, I want to shield myself and close my heart so I don't get hurt. It's too painful to get hurt. I don't want to. Despite all the pain and suffering in this world, there are countless wonders around me, wonders such as the smile of a child, the bloom of a flower, the rain, the morning dew, the leaves, the trees, the earth, and the sun. If I close my heart, I can't see all these wonders and beautiful things surrounding me. If I close my heart, I wouldn't be able to see all the helpers, the kindness of a random human being, the gentle breeze, and all the blessings in life. No, I want to keep my heart open, despite the risk of getting hurt and feeling pain. I want to sing, and dance, and praise life's wonders."

My teacher replied: "No Mud, No Lotus. Be a Lotus in the World."

As a busy professional, the pursuit of success often goes hand in hand with stress, anxiety, and a constant striving for more. In the midst of deadlines, meetings, and endless to-do lists, it's natural to feel overwhelmed by the weight of responsibility and the relentless pace of modern life. When facing many challenges, it's easy to succumb to negativity and see everything as doom and gloom. However, as Napoleon Bonaparte said, "Leaders are dealers of hope." Despite setbacks, as leaders in the workplace, we need to train ourselves to recognize the light and be open to opportunities to grow.

In the face of stress and adversity, mindfulness offers a sanctuary—a space to pause, breathe, and reconnect with the present moment. It invites us to acknowledge the mud—the struggles and imperfections of our lives—while also embracing the potential for growth, resilience, and beauty. Being a lotus in the world means embracing both the challenges and the wonders of our journey, recognizing that amid the chaos, there is beauty, growth, and the ever-present possibility of transformation.

NAVIGATE THE STORM AFTER LOSING A JOB

*"In the midst of change,
we often discover wings we never knew we had."
– Ekaterina Walter*

Expressing thoughts and emotions about job loss can be challenging, especially after experiencing it firsthand. In the past, I've focused on sharing insights about coping with job loss and maintaining a positive outlook. My expertise lies in engineering, leadership, and personal development coaching rather than career counseling. However, the prevalent job losses among my close circle, including my own, have prompted me to delve into this topic. Losing a job, regardless of mental preparedness, can be emotionally devastating, especially when one has invested their heart and soul into their work.

In the immediate aftermath of losing my job, I found myself with no energy despite believing I was mentally prepared for this scenario. The emotional toll was overwhelming, leading to days spent in tears, reminiscing about colleagues, and fretting over unfinished projects. The profound attachment to my job and the people I worked with intensified the impact of the loss. Although I outwardly claimed to be fine, the truth was that I struggled to carry on with normal activities, unable to eat or sleep. At one point, I found myself confiding in my husband about the insurmountable pain I was experiencing. I was unsure how to overcome it.

In an attempt to find solace, I turned to my "rescue" place—a Zen monastery. My journey with meditation has spanned over two decades, and I have consistently turned to this practice as a source of comfort and strength. This rescue place has been a cornerstone in my life, serving as a sanctuary where I seek refuge during moments of emotional upheaval. Its tranquil surroundings and the practice of meditation have been instrumental in guiding me through various trials, offering a sense of calm and clarity amid life's challenges. Here, in the tranquility of nature, I immersed myself in meditation.

Fortunately for me, there was a retreat the same weekend. The retreat began when the teacher shared a familiar yet forgotten story about salt and water. In the story, a teacher holds up a cup of water and adds several tablespoons of salt. He then asks whether the water is still drinkable, to which the response is no. The teacher then poses the question of what would happen if the same amount of salt were added to a river or a well. It becomes evident that the large volume of water in the river or well would dilute the salt, rendering it drinkable. The essence of the story lies in the analogy of the salt representing emotions and the water symbolizing one's capacity to hold those emotions. Instead of attempting to rid the water of the salt, which is impossible, the focus shifts to increasing the amount of water. By expanding one's capacity, just like the river diluting the salt, it becomes possible to accommodate and transform challenging emotions, thereby fostering resilience and emotional strength.

Engaging in prolonged periods of meditation, I initially struggled with persistent thoughts about the circumstances surrounding my job loss. Whenever my mind wandered, I would bring its attention back to my breathing, using the following verses: "Breathing in, I know I'm breathing in. Breathing out, I know I'm breathing out." Through focused breathing and mindfulness, I gradually anchored myself in the present moment, allowing the pain to coexist with an expanding sense of resilience.

Hours spent in silent contemplation, immersed in nature's beauty, gave me an appreciation for the profound blessings inherent in the present moment. Simple things like the blue sky, the birds' chirping, the green grass, the gentle wind, the sunshine, and my own breath, are blessings and wonders on earth.

The process of enlarging my capacity to endure and transform suffering became a pivotal facet of my healing journey. Like the analogy of the cup of water and the river, I came to realize that it is possible to expand one's ability to contain pain and adversity, ultimately transforming them into sources of strength and growth.

Thich Nhat Hanh once related, "One day, four children were playing at my Sweet Potato hermitage in France. Thanh Thuy, a four-year-old girl I was looking after, was among them. The children were thirsty, so I offered them each a glass of homemade apple juice. Thanh Thuy did not like the look of the cloudy juice and refused to drink it. She ran off to play but came back after a while and asked for water. I showed her the apple juice and urged her to drink it. She saw the pulp had settled, and the juice now looked clear and delicious. 'Is this the same glass or a different one?' she asked. 'Was it meditating like you?' I laughed. 'Let's say I am like the apple juice when I sit. That is closer to the truth.' If you know how to sit stably and follow your in-breath and out-breath, then after some time you become peaceful and clear, like the apple juice."

To those currently grappling with job loss, I empathize with the overwhelming nature of this experience. However, I urge you to remember that, like water in the cup and the river, you possess the inherent capacity to expand your resilience and to transform hardship into fortitude. If you can sit calmly and focus on your breathing, over time, you'll increase your ability to cope with suffering.

In sharing this deeply personal journey, I hope to inspire others to find solace and resilience as they navigate the challenging terrain of job loss and recovery.

LEARN TO PAUSE TO GROW

"In today's rush, we all think too much—seek too much —want too much—and forget about the joy of just being."
– Eckhart Tolle

This morning when I went out for my walk, the rain started pouring. Memories of my childhood in Vietnam flooded back. It rains a lot in Vietnam, a tropical country. Back then, rain meant more than just a change in weather; it meant a stop in the bustling city life, where bicycles and motorcycles were the primary mode of transportation. But since moving to the US, I've noticed a stark contrast. Here, cars dominate the roads, and rain fails to disrupt the constant motion of life. It seems everyone is caught up in a relentless pursuit, wearing busyness as a badge of honor.

Ask around, and you'll hear the same refrain: "I've been so busy," or "It's been nonstop." I, too, fell into this trap, equating busyness with self-worth. There's a lesson to be learned from the tale of the rider galloping through town who told onlookers to ask the horse where they were going. Are we, too, blindly chasing goals without pausing to consider their significance? What if our pursuits lead us astray, leaving us at the foot of the wrong ladder?

History's greatest leaders understood the power of pause. Nelson Mandela, during his twenty-seven years of imprisonment, found solace in reflection and personal growth. Marcus Aurelius, the Roman Emperor, extolled the virtues of journaling and meditation. And Mahatma Gandhi sought moral clarity through periods of silence. So, how can we incorporate pausing into our lives?

Create a Thinking Place and Time: Designate a space and time for reflection. Whether it's a quiet corner of your office or a bench in the park, make it a habit to visit regularly. It is like a pastor who finds solace atop a hill each morning, connecting, and conversing with God.

Practice Stillness: Spend a few moments in your thinking place, focusing on your breath and physical sensations. Count your breaths, feel the air around you, and tune in to your body and emotions. Without judgment, simply observe.

Reflect on Past Experiences: Consider challenging moments in your past and the lessons they taught you. What wisdom can you glean from adversity?

Envision Your Future: Picture where you want to be in the coming years. Visualize your goals as if they've already been achieved and identify the steps needed to reach them.

In a world that glorifies busyness, the power of pause offers a path to clarity and purpose. So, amid life's hustle and bustle, remember to pause, reflect, and chart your course with intention.

CONCLUSION

My work was stressful. It wasn't the work itself, but the environment. What used to be a great place to work had turned toxic after the company hired a senior leader who wrought havoc. He belittled others, believed in putting people down, and used intimidation. He constantly made up lies and accusations to discredit others, including my team and me. We were pushing deadlines and were understaffed. For close to a year, I was working more than a hundred hours a week, with little time for self-care or my family. For three months, I was traveling weekly, spending time on site, working close to sixteen hours a day. This was taking a toll on my nervous system. I felt tired most of the time and was always on the verge of crying. I slept only two to three hours nightly and had nightmares.

One day, I broke down and knew I had to return to my safe place—a meditation monastery in the US by the Plum Village tradition. I booked a room and a flight. As soon as I arrived, the peaceful energy of the place and the beautiful nature immediately calmed me down. I turned off my cellphone and tried my best to be present for the experience. I knew I needed this. For the first four days, I woke up at 2 a.m. in a sweat, having nightmares about the project at work. But on day five, things improved. I slept through the night. The schedule at the center left a lot of room for free time when we could rest, sleep, read, or sit in the garden. I usually sat in the garden. A couple of times, I visited the bookstore, and each time, I came out with a stack of books. Sister Dac Nghiem, the nun who worked in the bookstore, told me, "Thanh, stop reading, and start living. Be in the garden and just sit. Or sit in the meditation hall." She seemed to know exactly what I needed, even though we didn't talk much, and I kept to myself, never sharing the reason I came. But it was exactly what I needed. As I let my mind rest, gave myself a lot of space, and just sat in the present, I healed.

Mindfulness and meditation are not destinations. They are journeys and daily practices. As you pick up this practice and start implementing it in your daily life as a busy professional, you'll see its benefits. And if you, like me, happen to let go of the practice, don't sweat it. You can pick it up again here and now. Start living. Happiness is here and now.

With love,
Thanh Nguyen

NOTES

Scientific Evidence on the Benefits of Mindfulness

[1] Goldin, P. R., & Gross, J. J. (2010). Effects of mindfulness-based stress reduction (MBSR) on emotion regulation in social anxiety disorder. *Emotion*, 10(1), 83–91.

[2] Goyal, M., Singh, S., Sibinga, E. M. S., Gould, N. F., Rowland-Seymour, A., Sharma, R., ... & Ranasinghe, P. D. (2014). Meditation programs for psychological stress and well-being: A systematic review and meta-analysis. *JAMA Internal Medicine*, 174(3), 357–368.

[3] Zeidan, F., Johnson, S. K., Diamond, B. J., David, Z., & Goolkasian, P. (2010). Mindfulness meditation improves cognition: Evidence of brief mental training. *Consciousness and Cognition*, 19(2), 597–605.

[4] Keng, S. L., Smoski, M. J., & Robins, C. J. (2011). Effects of mindfulness on psychological health: A review of empirical studies. *Clinical Psychology Review*, 31(6), 1041–1056.

[5] Hölzel, B. K., Carmody, J., Vangel, M., Congleton, C., Yerramsetti, S. M., Gard, T., & Lazar, S. W. (2011). Mindfulness practice leads to increases in regional brain gray matter density. *Psychiatry Research: Neuroimaging*, 191(1), 36–43.

[6] Hilton, L., Hempel, S., Ewing, B. A., Apaydin, E., Xenakis, L., Newberry, S., ... & Maglione, M. A. (2017). Mindfulness meditation for chronic pain: Systematic review and meta-analysis. *Annals of Behavioral Medicine*, 51(2), 199–213.

ABOUT THE AUTHOR

Thanh was originally from Vietnam but later immigrated to the United States during her teenage years. During this time, she faced financial struggles, language barriers and even abuse from her caretaker.

However, after several decades, Thanh achieved two graduate degrees, one in electrical engineering and the other in business administration. She holds two United States patents, gained over twenty years of experience in corporate America, and served as Vice President of Engineering at a prominent engineering procurement construction firm.

As a certified coach, teacher, and speaker of John Maxwell Leadership Team, as well as a long-time practitioner of mindfulness, Thanh strongly believes in the power of the right mindset and support system to overcome challenges and make a positive impact. She is passionate about helping individuals thrive by sharing stories and techniques that foster a positive mindset and inspire courageous actions.

Thanh co-founded The Encourage Team to offer leadership and personal development, empowering people to live positively and lead courageously. Connect with Thanh and embark on this journey of reflection, self-discovery, and accelerated growth.

SUGGESTED READING

Peace Is Every Step: The Path of Mindfulness in Everyday Life by Thich Nhat Hanh

You Are Here: Discover the Magic of the Present Moment by Thich Nhat Hanh

The Miracle of Mindfulness: An Introduction to the Practice of Meditation by Thich Nhat Hanh

No Mud, No Lotus: The Art of Transforming Suffering by Thich Nhat Hanh

10% Happier: How I Tamed the Voice in My Head, Reduced Stress Without Losing My Edge, and Found Self-Help That Actually Works — a True Story by Dan Harris

The Untethered Soul: The Journey Beyond Yourself by Michael A. Singer

The Power of Now: A Guide to Spiritual Enlightenment by Eckhart Tolle

Think Like a Monk: Train Your Mind for Peace and Purpose Every Day by Jay Shetty

The Art of Happiness by the Dalai Lama

When Things Fall Apart: Heart Advice for Difficult Times by Pema Chödrön

Wherever You Go, There You Are: Mindfulness Meditation in Everyday Life by Jon Kabat-Zinn

Real Happiness: The Power of Meditation by Sharon Salzberg

The 7 Habits of Highly Effective People by Stephen R. Covey

How Will You Measure Your Life? by Clayton M. Christensen

Man's Search for Meaning by Viktor E. Frankl

"Every time we need the energy of mindfulness, we just touch that seed with our mindful breathing, and then we have the energy ready to do the work of recognizing, embracing, and transforming."
– Thich Nhat Hanh

www.ingramcontent.com/pod-product-compliance
Lightning Source LLC
Chambersburg PA
CBHW060341130626
46553CB00003B/1072